My Path to Heaven

A young person's guide to the Faith

My Path to Heaven

A young person's guide to the Faith

by Geoffrey Bliss, S.J.

Illustrations
by
Caryll Houselander

Sophia Institute Press®
Manchester, New Hampshire

Sophia Institute Press®
Box 5284, Manchester, NH 03108
1-800-888-9344

Nihil Obstat: Ernest Messenger, Ph.D., Censor Deputatus
Imprimatur: Joseph Butt. Vic. Gen.
Westmonasterii, April 15, 1936

Library of Congress Cataloging-in-Publication Data

Bliss, Geoffrey, b. 1874.
     [Retreat with Saint Ignatius]
     My path to heaven : a young person's guide to the faith / by Geoffrey Bliss ; illustrations
          by Caryll Houselander.
          p.   cm.
     Originally published: A retreat with Saint Ignatius. New York : Sheed & Ward, 1936.
     Summary: Twelve lessons focus on important teachings of the Catholic faith, including our
          relationship with God, the consequences of sin, and events in the life of Jesus.
     ISBN 0-918477-48-4 (pbk. : alk. paper)
     1. Children — Prayer-books and devotions — English. 2. Catholic Church — Doctrines —
          Juvenile literature. 3. Christian life — Catholic authors — Juvenile literature.
          4. Children — Religious life. [1. Catholic Church — Doctrines. 2. Christian life.
          3. Prayer books and devotions.] I. Houselander, Caryll, ill. II. Title.
     BX2150.B45 1997
     248.8'2 — dc21   97-13452   CIP
                                                                                                              AC

97 98 99 00 01 10 9 8 7 6 5 4 3 2

Contents

My Path to Heaven

A young person's guide to the Faith

How to Read This Book

This book is based on the SPIRITUAL EXERCISES of St. Ignatius of Loyola.[1] It is divided into twelve parts. Each part shows a picture and tells what the picture is about. Study only one picture each day.

1. When you begin to read this book, look first of all at the first picture. Look all over it, just long enough to get curious as to what it is all about.

2. Then read the print on the pages that follow the picture. Read all of this explanation very slowly; it would be better to read it twice.

3. Next, turn back to the picture and look at it for as long as you like. There may be some things in the picture you still don't understand. So read the explanation once more.

4. Then read the "yes or no" questions and see if you can answer them all. When you're not sure whether the answer is a yes or a no, ask a grown-up.

---

[1] St. Ignatius (1491-1556) founded the Society of Jesus.

5. When you say your night prayers, think for a minute about the picture, and tell God what you think.

This book was made especially for the child Crusaders of the Apostleship of Prayer (or League of the Sacred Heart of Jesus).[2] You will see that crusaders are sometimes mentioned in the explanations and shown in the pictures.

---

[2] Crusaders are soldiers for Jesus. They help Him in the battle to fight sin and save souls. They are shown with crosses on their clothes.

God made me for Himself, and
He made all other things to get me to Him.

Made for God

The young boy at the bottom of the picture is supposed to be just made, or created, by God; that is why two lines come down from God's hands onto his head.

God has told the angels to get him ready to do what God made him for. This is because whatever God makes, He makes it for something — just as we do. If we make a dress, it is to wear, and that settles the shape; if we make a knife, it is to cut. If a knife is well made, it is sure to cut, because it has no choice about it; but the boy in the picture is not sure to do what he was made for, because he has a choice; he is free.

God made me to love Him

This boy was made to love God; and in order to love, you must be free: that means you must be able to say: "I will not love." The stars can't love God, who made them so beautiful, because they are not free.

In order to love God, you must know Him and honor Him and do His will. This boy was made to do all that and, by doing that, to save his soul and go to Heaven and be happy with God forever.

God made all other things to help me love Him

And now, what about all the other things God has made? All the powers this boy has in his body and in his soul? And all the things he comes across during his life: the sun and moon and stars and animals and trees and flowers? And all the things the boy will feel: joys and sorrows, troubles and good fortune, friendship and loneliness, being ill and being well, and temptations and graces? And all the things the boy will do: eating and sleeping and walking and talking and working and studying and playing? Did God make all these things too? Yes, of course. And what for? Here is the wonderful answer: all to help that boy to do what he was made for, to love God and save his soul.

Yes, whatever you come across during your life, God made it, and that is what He meant to make it for: just to help you to love Him with your own free choice.

Faith leads me to God

When you have finished reading this and go back to look at the picture, you will see all these things, and the boy doing them or coming across them. You can recognize him everywhere by the candle he holds. That candle is the gift of Faith, and it keeps reminding him why he is doing all the things he does: that is, to love God and save his soul.

In the picture, you will see him eating and sleeping and warming him-self, and going into the dark. You will see him working and studying, playing and watching the animals, and listening to music. You will see him laughing at himself all alone by himself (down in the right-hand corner) and searching out God's wonderful works (near the top): with a telescope, like the scientists, or just looking up and thinking about them, like the poets. You will see him fighting one devil and running away from another; you will see him sick or wounded with an angel by him; and you will see him praying. You will see him sometimes all alone and sometimes with companions or a friend.

But all the time, he is going up the stairs to God. At their very top, the low, wide doorway between the cypress trees is the gateway out of this life, which is called death. Higher up again you see the boy, very small, still with his candle of Faith, flying back to God, who made him.

Yes or No?

1. Did God make you?

2. Does He want you?

3. Does He want you because He loves you?

4. Are you able to eat and sleep and walk and play?

5. Is this what God made you for?

6. Is there some one thing God made you to do?

7. Is it something that stones and stars
and plants and animals can't do?

8. Is it to love?

9. Is it to love just anything?

10. Is it to love God?

11. Can you love God without knowing Him?

12. Can you love God if you don't try
to please and obey Him?

(8 yeses and 4 noes)

The best way of life is the one
that will take me to Heaven.

The Best Way of Life

There are so many different ways of life. Some people have a long life, and some a short life. Some are rich, and some are poor. Some are healthy, and some are often sick, or they are crippled or blind. Some are grand folk who get a lot of honor and praise; many live plain, simple lives, and nobody knows anything about them, and some may even fall into disgrace without much fault of their own. Some have lots of friends, and some are lonely. Some are single, and some are married. Some are clever and quick at learning, and others are slow. And a life may change from one kind to another, like going through different towns on a journey.

Which of these different kinds of lives is the best for me? Which should I want to have? Is it better (for me) to be rich or to be poor? Is it better to be healthy or to be ill?

Perhaps you are almost ready to laugh at these questions. You say, "Oh! I know the answer to that; of course it's better to be healthy and rich."

But wait a minute. Here is a different question: Which is the best train to take from London if you want to go to Liverpool? Why, the train that goes there, I suppose! And if there are many, then the train that goes the quickest and straightest way.

All lives lead to Heaven or to Hell

Well, now, where are all those different kinds of lives going to? For they don't go on forever. They are all going to Heaven or else to Hell. Now, which life (for me) is the best? I can hear you all answer at once: "Oh! the life that goes to Heaven is best, and the surer it is to get me there, the better it is!"

Then let us try again. Is it better to be rich or poor? Suppose (it's rather a funny thing to imagine) that a poor man knew that being poor was taking him to Hell; should he try to get rich? Yes! If he was sure, he should! And suppose a rich man knew that his riches were taking him to Hell; should he try hard to get rid of his riches and be poor? Yes, indeed he should.

I should choose the life that will lead me to Heaven

Well, that is the great lesson of this part of the book. Any kind of life can take a man to Heaven, although some kinds (such as lives of honor and riches) very seldom do, and they are very crooked roads! But the only question worth asking about all of them is: "Will this kind of life take me to Heaven?" If it will, it is the best; if not, it is the worst, however nice the name of it sounds.

The picture is rather like a sort of map. All the roads go to Heaven and to Hell; and they go through all sorts of places with the names of the different kinds of lives. Sometimes I can choose my own road; but generally God chooses it for me, and then I know it is a good road for me, if I keep in the right direction. Of course, Heaven is much more lovely and Hell much more dreadful than they are in the picture.

✂

Yes or No?

1. If you manage to love God right, does it matter
what else happens to you on earth?

2. Is a long life always better than a short one?

3. Is it better to be rich than to be poor?

4. Is it always better to be well than to be ill?

5. Is it always better to be ill than to be well?

6. Does it all depend?

7. Does it depend on which helps you most to love God?

8. Does it depend on anything else?

9. Then should you want to be rich and healthy
and live long, regardless of whether all
that will help you to love God or not?

10. Is the best kind of life the kind that you can use
best to get to God and save your soul?

11. Are these retreat pictures meant just to amuse you?

12. When you look at them, should you think
about God and your soul all the time?

(4 yeses and 8 noes)

Sin is the only evil. It ruined some
of the angels and Adam and may ruin me.

The Three Sins

Remembering that God made all the angels and us men, and what He made them for — that is, to love Him — now we look to see what they did, whether they did love Him or not. For, remember, you can't love (any more than a stone can) unless you are free not to love.

Some angels sinned against God

First we look at the angels (on the right-hand side of the picture). The angels were made so strong and so beautiful by God that when an angel came to St. John with a message, St. John thought, at first, that it was God Himself.

At the top of the right-hand side of the picture are a few of the angels who fell from Heaven.[3] You see what they are doing: they are admiring their own beauty as if it were their doing; they are thinking of themselves and loving themselves, not God. The moment their love was tested (perhaps by being shown a vision of the Baby Jesus and told they must adore Him and honor his Mother as their Queen), they rebelled. They said, "I won't serve." This was because they wouldn't love.

---

[3] Luke 10:18; Revelation 12:7-9.

It was a fearful sin, for they did it with all their might, never to change, once and for all, forever! And you know what that sin did to them: it changed them from false lovers into true haters, from angels into devils, who hated everything good and loved only evil; it made them cruel, cowardly, and foul. If we want to know what sin is, we can tell by what comes of it.

Adam and Eve sinned against God

For the second sin, look at the left-hand side of the picture. God made Adam and Eve as perfect as ever He could. And then He gave them special gifts they had no right to. He made them full of grace, like you just after your Baptism. Then they couldn't get angry or greedy or lazy without noticing it, like us, but only by wishing to. And they could never get ill. Also, although it was natural for them to die, God said, "You never shall die; after you have proved your love of me, I will lift you up to Heaven to live with me and the good angels. To prove your love, don't eat the fruit on that one tree."

Well, Eve ate the fruit because the chief fallen angel said she would be "like God," knowing all things, if she did; and then Adam ate, too. It was a terrible sin, because they knew so well how good God had been to them, and because their souls were made so strong and wise. They began to be ashamed and repent almost at once because they were not so mighty as the bad angels.[4]

But sin had got into the world, and what did it do? The rest of the left side of the picture — and all the middle part — tells you. One sin brought

---

[4] *Genesis 2:17 and 3:1-10.*

more sin (Cain's wicked murder of Abel),[5] and it brought death and sickness and sorrow and labor and suffering into the world, and these have gone flowing through the world like a huge river ever since. The center of the picture shows this. If we want to know what sin is, we can tell by what comes of it.

I sin against God

The third sin is my sin if, in the end, I do what the bad angels and Adam did and do not repent like Adam. In the picture, you can see among the devils at the bottom of Hell one human figure, and you can say: that might be me. Perhaps I would be there if God had not been patient and given me so much grace. We can tell what sin is by what comes of it.

Jesus died for my sins

Now look at the very top left-hand corner of the picture, and see Jesus Christ, true God and true Man, dying on the Cross for my sins. And think: "This is what Jesus, my God, has done for me. What have I done for Him up to now? What am I doing for Him? What am I going to do for Him?" And this is the time to speak to Jesus and tell Him the thoughts you have in your heart. Then look at the figure of sinless Mary, opposite, and ask her to pray for you.

---

[5] *Genesis 4:2-8.*

Yes or No?

1. Is sin a great evil?

2. Is there anything else besides sin that is altogether evil?

3. Is it our memory or understanding that we sin with?

4. Is it our free will?

5. Can plants and animals sin against God?

6. Is this because they do not have our free will?

7. Does our free will make us higher than all God's other creatures except the angels?

8. Did God give us free will to do what we like with it?

9. Did He give it to us to love Him with?

10. Is every sin something done against God's love and goodness?

11. Does sin spoil and ruin the sinner?

12. Did it change angels into devils?

13. Did it change Adam's happiness into misery?

14. Did it bring into the world all the unhappiness there is now?

15. Would we have had to die before going to live with God if there had been no sin?

(10 yeses and 5 noes)

God has done all He can for me,
and yet I have sinned against Him.

My Own Sins

After seeing, by the sin of the angels and Adam, what a horrible thing sin is, I apply this to my life by thinking about my own sins. (If, by God's kind grace, you have kept your soul clear of any big sins until now, you can think of what you would be like if you had given in to the Devil, or of what you will be like if this ever happens.)

So I say: "I am like Job sitting all alone on his dunghill, with sores and ulcers all over me — but his sores were clean and nice compared with my sin-sores."[6] And I look back on my life and see how those sores have been getting worse and worse. I think what a shameful and foul thing any mortal sin (such as gluttony or hatred) is, even if it wasn't forbidden by God.

God is infinitely greater than I am

Then I think about how small and worthless I am. What am I compared with all the other people in the world? Couldn't God have easily gotten along without me? He has thousands and thousands of holy, lovely angels and saints with Him already in Heaven. Then I say: "And even all angels and all men are like nothing compared with God; so what am I before

---

[6] Job 2:7-8. Job was a man known for his patience in suffering. His story is in the Old Testament.

God's holy majesty?" And I begin to look at my sores, which are my sins, and think how nasty and filthy sin has made me all over.

Then I think of God, whom I have sinned against, and I try to compare myself with Him. He knows all things, and I know hardly anything; He is all-powerful, and there is scarcely anything good I can do by myself; He is just, and I am unjust: to Him and to my neighbor and to myself; He is good, and I am bad when I sin against Him.

God is kind and patient

After thinking of all this for some time, I begin to feel very astonished that God should be so kind to me and so patient; and that He should let all His servants, all His creatures, be kind to me too! The very angels and saints in Heaven are sorry for me and are praying for me for the grace to repent of my sins. And all God's world around me is giving me life and food and comfort. God's sun shines on me; His clean air comes into my body to keep me alive; His wonderful plants and animals supply me with my food. All these things are the innocent servants of God; I ought to be surprised that they can be so good to me when I sin so against God.

I can turn to God in sorrow when I sin

By now I feel so sorry and so ashamed of my sins that I don't know what to say or where to go. But where can I go but to God? So I go to Him, all full of sorrow and shame; and tell Him all my thoughts (which He knows already); and show Him the sores of my sins. And I thank Him from the bottom of my heart for loving me so much that He could be patient with me. I thank Him for giving me my life up to now in spite of my sins. I promise Him that, with His grace, I will hate sin in the future and love goodness, and be His innocent and faithful child. Then I end by saying some little prayers to Jesus crucified and to Mary, the Refuge of Sinners.

Yes or No?

1. Can sin ruin me and make me fit to be a
companion of devils in Hell?

2. Are sins ugly and foul even if they have not been forbidden?

3. Does God have many holy angels and saints to praise
Him and love Him, who did not sin against Him?

4. Am I a very important creature of God, who has
so many creatures and can make as many as He will?

5. Could He do without me?

6. Am I wise or great or good compared with God, or compared
with many other of God's creatures?

7. Did God stop being good to me when I sinned against Him?

8. Did He let His creatures, the sun and the air and the animals and
the plants, go on being good to me and feeding me?

9. Did God, after I had sinned, give His own
Son to die for me on the Cross?

10. Should I be full of shame and sorrow for sins against God?

11. Should I speak to our Lady at the foot of the Cross about my sins?

12. Should I speak to Jesus on the Cross about them?

13. Shall I ask myself what I am doing now
for Jesus to make up for sins?

14. Shall I ask myself what I am going to do in the future?

(12 yeses and 2 noes)

Jesus calls you to fight by His side.

How do you answer Him?

The Call of a King

When you look at the picture this time, you will see that there are two pictures, one laid on top of the other. Don't look at the top one yet, but look at the one below it, which goes all around the edge of the other. And look at the lower part of it and at the middle of this part. What do you see there? You see a king. You notice he is wounded. What is he doing? He is giving a welcome to some knights or soldiers who have come to promise to follow him and to fight faithfully under him as their leader. They are taking the oath of fealty. The king has the blessing of Holy Church upon him; you see a bishop standing nearby.

What is the king fighting for? The rest of the picture (around the edges of the top picture) tells you that. You see a great, fortified town full of pagans adoring idols; these pagans have threatened to come out of their city and conquer all the Christian countries. The king is going to stop that and capture their town.

What would you say to the king in the picture if he asked you to fight on his side? Suppose he said to you: "It will be a very stern fight and last a long time, but I promise you victory in the end; and you will find me always in the very front line, fighting along with you. Will you follow me? I need faithful followers." What would you answer?

Jesus calls me to fight sin and the Devil with Him

Well, all this is "suppose" and imagining. But now look at the top picture. In this picture what we imagined has come true! There is Jesus Christ, bearing His Cross. He is a king. And today He is still fighting a great fight against sin and the Devil and all "the powers of darkness."[7] And He wants followers — as many as He can get. He asks men to follow Him and fight along with Him. He asks you. He says to you: "The fight will be hard and will last all your life. But you will not have to suffer anything that I do not bear too; I shall be close at your side in the fight. And I promise you victory in the end. You will save your own soul from sin and the Devil and make it part of my kingdom; and then you will help to save many other souls. Will you come with me? I want you for my follower."

How are you going to answer Jesus Christ? For this is not a "suppose," but is true. And although you are still a child, you are old enough to answer and take your solemn vow of fealty to Jesus Christ. And He is waiting for your answer. If we are not base, dishonorable cowards, there is only one way we can answer the call of Christ the King: by promising to be loyal followers, ready to fight bravely, at all cost, every evil thing that is an enemy of Jesus.

Following Jesus means suffering with Him

But there are some who make an even better answer to the King's call and say: "Jesus, my Lord, let me fight very close beside You and have a special share in all the hard things You Yourself suffered in this fight, even if it means being as poor as You, and disgraced as You were, and persecuted."

---

[7] Colossians 1:13.

If you look at the center picture again, you will see that the followers of Jesus have not taken swords for their weapons, but crosses. Those who follow Jesus must suffer more or less, and be patient in suffering. Jesus said, "If you will come after me, deny yourself, take up your cross daily, and follow me."[8]

The center picture shows Bethlehem and Nazareth and Calvary to remind us of the places where Jesus was born in poverty, and was subject to St. Joseph, and "went about doing good,"[9] and "had not where to lay His head,"[10] and fought against sin and the Devil, and was persecuted and crucified.[11] Up above you see the new heavenly Jerusalem, where the King will reign in glory with his followers forever. Below, some of His enemies are shown: men who (like the Pharisees then[12] and others now) make themselves the friends of the enemies of Jesus.

Think well about the answer you mean to make to the call of Jesus Christ the King.

---

[8] Luke 9:23.

[9] Acts 10:38.

[10] Matthew 8:20; Luke 9:58.

[11] Chapter 2 of Luke's Gospel tells about Jesus' birth and childhood. You can read about Jesus' crucifixion on Calvary in Matthew 27:33-50, Mark 15:22-37, Luke 23:33-46, and John 19:17-30.

[12] The Pharisees were a Jewish religious group who followed the law very exactly. Many of them criticized Jesus for such acts as forgiving sins, being kind to sinners, and healing on the Sabbath. See Matthew 23:13-36 and Luke 18:9-14.

✂

Yes or No?

1. If you were grown up, and a great king asked you to join his army to fight against some cruel and wicked people who were trying to kill all the good people, would you run away and hide?

2. Would you say yes?

3. Would you think anyone who was strong and well, but said no, was a coward?

4. Is there really a king who does ask you to fight along with him?

5. Is this king Jesus Christ?

6. Is it the Devil and all the "powers of darkness" that He is fighting against?

7. In the fight, will you have to suffer more than Jesus the King has suffered Himself?

8. Are you certain to win if you are loyal and faithful?

9. Does Jesus the King wish to conquer a kingdom?

10. Is it a kingdom of this world?

11. Is it your own soul?

12. Does He have a right to be king there?

13. Can you conquer your own soul for Jesus without helping to conquer other souls for Him?

(9 yeses and 4 noes)

The Son of God became man to save
men from sin and lead them to Heaven.

The Incarnation

Now that we have promised to follow Jesus Christ and fight for His kingdom, we wish to know who He is, and where He came from, and where He leads us. So we begin with His coming, in the great mystery of the Incarnation.

The Blessed Trinity is one God in three Persons

At the top of the picture you see God, the most Blessed Trinity, which "always was and is and always will be": the eternal Father; and His eternal Son, begotten of the Father, who is like the Father in all things; and the Holy Spirit, who "proceeds," or comes forth, from the Father and the Son and is the eternal Love between Them.

All people share in Adam's sin

You see the Blessed Trinity looking down upon the round world full of men, which the Blessed Trinity created out of love. It is two thousand years ago, and you see all the men and women in the world then, all the different peoples, drawn very small: the Egyptians and the Greeks and the Romans; the Eskimos and the American Indians and the ancient Britons; the Chinese and the Japanese; and the South Sea Islanders and the Africans. And none of them know anything about God, although they are enjoying all the good things He has given them; when they pray, they pray to the sun or to the moon or to idols, and not to God; they commit sins, and they do not know how to repent of them.

What makes them so ignorant and so wretched? It is the great sin of Adam, which you thought about in the third picture. They are all Adam's children and share in his disgrace and his loss of God's friendship; and so Heaven is closed to them; and the pit of Hell — the prison house of those other rebels against God, the wicked angels — is waiting for them. But God, the Blessed Trinity, still loves them; and now the Three Divine Persons are planning how to save them and how to enable them to make up for Adam's sin and their own sins.

Imagine that the Father said: "The ignorant prayers and sacrifices of men are not pleasing to me. Adam sinned against me, and they have all sinned, and there is not one that perfectly obeys or loves me." And then imagine that the Son said: "Father, I will go down to them, and I will take their nature upon me, and I will obey Thee and love Thee perfectly; and I will teach them also how to love Thee; and I will take their sins upon me, and I will make myself a sacrifice for their sins!"

The Second Person of the Blessed Trinity became man

And the Father "so loved men" that He consented to give His only-begotten Son;[13] and the Holy Spirit, the Love between the Father and the Son, consented; and the angel Gabriel was sent down to Mary in Nazareth, and the Holy Spirit breathed upon her; and in her, God the Son was made

---

[13] John 3:16.

man, having a body and soul like ours, and was born a little child in the stable at Bethlehem.[14]

He had a humble virgin for His mother, and only poor shepherds to greet Him, and only straw to lie upon; because He was beginning already to make His great sacrifice, and to teach us how to love God better than riches or pleasure or having our own way.

Jesus came to save the world

In the picture, in a cave under the world, you see Adam and Eve. They are looking at the Cross, which will save men from the results of their sin in the garden.[15] The serpent on the Cross is not the wicked serpent who tempted them; it is the "brazen serpent" that God told Moses to set up in the desert when snakes attacked the Israelites, and all who looked at it were safe.[16] This brazen serpent was a figure or symbol of Jesus Christ on the Cross, because He took on Himself the sins of men and died for them.[17]

Look at the picture, and thank God with all your whole heart for His wonderful loving kindness and mercy.

[14] Luke 1:26-35 and 2:7.

[15] Genesis 3:6.

[16] Numbers 21:5-9.

[17] John 3:14-15.

✣

Yes or No?

1. Did Jesus Christ come into the world grown up, dressed
like a great king, with angels to wait on Him?

2. Did He come as a little baby, born of the
Virgin Mary in a stable?

3. Was this the best way for Him to come?

4. Was it the best way because He came to save us
from pride and disobedience?

5. Was He in Heaven from all eternity before He came?

6. Did His Father, the First Person of the Blessed
Trinity, give Him to us?

7. Did the Holy Spirit create a human soul and
body for Him, to be His own?

8. Could Jesus feel and suffer just as we do?

9. Could we ever have made up for our sins
if He had not come?

10. Did He come to save only the Jews?

11. Did He come to save all men?

12. Can we ever thank God enough for the
mystery of the Incarnation?

(8 yeses and 4 noes)

Satan says: greed, vainglory, pride.

Christ says: poverty, contempt, humility.

The Two Standards

This picture shows two camps, divided by a narrow river flowing between high cliffs. The left-hand camp is the camp of the Devil, where he is urging on his followers, the other devils, and commanding them to use a certain plan to ruin men and prevent them from following Christ, and to bring them to Hell. His plan is shown on the standard, or banner, he holds.

Satan's standard: greed, vainglory, pride

"First," Satan says, "make them greedy to have things: money and comfort and everything money can buy; then make them wish to be honored and looked up to and envied and praised by others; then make them proud, thinking a great deal of themselves. Once you have made them proud, you can easily get them to commit all sorts of sins."

So the Devil's standard has on it GREED, VAINGLORY, PRIDE. And these are the nets and chains with which you see the devils catching and binding men in the picture. The city at the top is "Babylon,"[18] or the "world" that the catechism means when it speaks of "the world, the flesh, and the

---

[18] Babylon was an ancient city of wicked people who wanted only to please themselves.

Devil."[19] This city, or world, is full of the slaves the Devil has captured and hopes to bring at last to his own place, Hell.

Christ's standard: poverty, contempt, humility

On the other side of the picture is the camp of Jesus Christ. He is not sitting on a great throne, like Satan. He is not giving out angry orders, but whispering His advice gently to His followers, to show them how to save men and bring them to Him, and so get them to Heaven. His standard is the Cross. And it has three words on it, like Satan's. The words are POVERTY, CONTEMPT, HUMILITY. They show what the advice is that Jesus gives to those who wish to help Him to save men's souls.

"First," He says, "teach them to go without unnecessary things and to be content; tell them always to be ready to give up what they have for God's sake and their souls' sake. Then encourage them not to hunger for praise, but to be brave enough to bear others' laughter, scorn, and contempt. Lastly, make them humble, remembering that all they have is given to them by God. When you have made them humble, you can easily teach them all other virtues." Jesus, who gives these directions to His subjects, followed them Himself in His life on earth.

The city at the top of the picture is the city, or kingdom, of God, and those who live in it are the true followers and imitators of Jesus Christ.

The three pairs of men

Do you intend to be captured by the Devil by his threefold plan? Or will you join the camp of Jesus Christ and follow His threefold plan? For we

---

[19] From the BOOK OF COMMON PRAYER, the Litany.

must do one or the other. To help us to choose wisely and bravely, St. Ignatius shows us "The Three Pairs of Men." You can see it in the lower part of the picture. You see three very narrow bridges going across the gulf from Satan's camp to Christ's. The three pairs of men, wishing to leave Satan and go to Christ, have arrived at the bridges, each pair with a donkey cart piled high with ducats, which means pieces of gold money. (And that stands for anything that might keep you from following Jesus Christ.)

The first pair, nearest you, are sitting on the ducats and talking about whether they should leave their ducats behind and walk over the bridge; and they go on considering and putting it off until they die. The devils are quite content with these men. The second pair are determined to get into Christ's camp, but not without the ducats; so, as the bridge is too narrow for the cart, they begin to pack the ducats into small baskets in which to carry them across; the devils are pretending to help but are really hindering; at the other end of the bridge stands Time, warning the men that they may be too late. The last pair make no delay; they let the donkey go, leave the cart, and walk over the bridge. The devils are very angry with these two men.

Make up your mind which pair of men you will be like when something seems to be keeping you from following Jesus Christ immediately and perfectly.

Yes or No?

1. Does the Devil make war on Jesus Christ and His followers?

2. Does the Devil have an army of devils, and of men too, to help him?

3. Does he sit on a high throne, giving out fierce orders?

4. Does he have a plan for his wicked fight?

5. Is it a threefold plan?

6. Does he begin by getting people to want to have more and more money and things you can buy with it?

7. Then does he try to make them want to be admired?

8. Then does he try to make them proud?

9. When he has made them proud, is it difficult for him to make them commit many other sins?

10. Does Jesus Christ have an army too?

11. Does He give fierce orders from a high throne?

12. Does He whisper His advice gently to His followers?

13. Does He have a threefold plan also?

14. Does He begin by getting His followers not to mind being poor?

15. Then does He advise them to be willing to be ignored and thought little of?

16. In this way, does He make them humble?

17. Is it easy for them, then, to get other virtues?

18. If something prevents you from following Jesus, should you say you will get rid of it at some time or another?

19. Should you say: I will find out how to keep this thing and yet follow Jesus too?

20. Should you give the thing up at once?

(16 yeses and 4 noes)

I must choose my state of life
according to God's glory and my salvation.

The Election

This is why St. Ignatius especially wrote his SPIRITUAL EXERCISES: to help anyone to choose the kind of life he ought to live; whether to go on living as he did before, or to change. Sometimes young men or women (not long out of school) have to choose a state of life: perhaps whether to take up some particular kind of work or business, or not; perhaps whether to marry someone in particular, or not; perhaps whether to become a priest or religious, or not. A Christian cannot make a choice like this without thinking about God and about his soul. So St. Ignatius advises him how to think.

There are three degrees of humility

And first of all, he tells him to think about "Three Degrees (or steps) of Humility." The first is when you have enough humility before God to be able to say no at once if you are offered some great fortune on the condition that you commit one mortal sin against God. The second is when you would not dream of committing even one venial sin to win some great prize. The third is a very perfect humility: when you don't want money and praise even if you could have them without any sin, but instead you want to be like Jesus Christ in His humiliation and in His sufferings. These three degrees are shown at the top of the big picture.

I must weigh my reasons

Now look at the main part of the picture. The crusader has a box on his lap. In it is the state of life he is wondering whether to choose or not. (The keyhole is like a question mark to show his uncertainty.) He is sitting right in the middle of a big weighing machine, and he wants to weigh his reasons for taking this state of life or leaving it. (You see the words TAKE and LEAVE on the scale pans.) First of all, he has wisely put all his weights into two piles, separating the false weights from the true. (The piles of weights are drawn big so that you can read their names.)

I must choose whatever is for God's glory and my soul's salvation

He wants to choose what will give glory to God. Around the picture of God, in the big circle over the crusader's head, run the words AD MAJOREM DEI GLORIAM. These words mean "for the greater glory of God." And the crusader wants to choose what will help him to save his soul. Under the picture of God are more Latin words, ET ANIMAE SALUTEM, which mean "and for my soul's salvation." The little clouds and flames are the crusader's thoughts and prayers going up to God.

Now, suppose he is choosing whether to be a priest or not; he might take the true weight labeled APOSTLESHIP, which means "saving souls," and put it into the scale pan marked TAKE. But suppose he has an elderly mother who needs him to help her; he would take another true weight (not shown in the picture) labeled DUTY TO PARENTS and put it into the other scale pan marked LEAVE; and I think that pan would be the heavier.

I must consider three things before I weigh my choices

But it is not always so easy to use the true weights; and even if you do, you may make mistakes in the weighing because you are not quite honest in your mind. So St. Ignatius tells you to think three thoughts before you begin to weigh; and these three thoughts are shown in three smaller circles around the crusader. The first (on your left) is the thought of how he will wish he had chosen when he is dying. The second (on your right) is what he will wish he had chosen when his soul comes before God all alone to be judged. The third (just under the crusader) is how he would advise another person, not himself, about choosing this state of life, if he was asked to advise him.

And, of course, all the time you are weighing, you must pray and remember that God, our Lady, and all the saints are watching you.

A good choice can be made in three ways

This great election, or choosing, is not always made by this way of carefully weighing our reasons for and against. There are three times, altogether, when a good choice can be made, and they are shown in the three little pictures underneath the main picture. One time is when God makes the choice for a man and calls him, as he called St. Matthew from his money table.[20] Another time is when a man goes through temptations, and gets graces, hearing the whispers of the Devil and the whispers of his guardian angel, until he knows clearly what he ought to do to please God. And the third way is by thinking quietly and weighing reasons, as we have seen.

---

[20] Matthew 9:9.

⚮

Yes or No?

1. Is it a high kind of humility before God if you would not commit a mortal sin against Him for some big reward?

2. Is it a higher kind if you would not commit a deliberate venial sin to get a great fortune?

3. Is it the highest kind if you don't want any big reward, but want to share in the suffering and humiliation of Jesus Christ?

4. Is there any choice more important than the choice of a state of life?

5. Does God sometimes choose a state for a man and call him to it clearly?

6. Can a man sometimes tell how to choose by hearing the Devil tempt him, and his good angel giving him good advice in his soul?

7. Is the ordinary way to choose by thinking of reasons and weighing them to see which are heaviest?

8. Is the first great reason for choosing always: What will give the most glory to God and make me most sure to save my soul?

9. Will it help me to find this out to think: What shall I wish I had chosen when I am dying?

10. Will it help to think: What shall I wish I had chosen when I am being judged after death?

11. Will it help to think: What would I advise another person to choose if he asked me to help him to make a good choice?

12. When I weigh the reasons for choosing, can I use any weights I like?

13. Are there such things as false weights?

14. Are COMFORT and SUCCESS true weights?

15. Is DUTY TO PARENTS a true weight?

(11 yeses and 4 noes)

Jesus Christ takes on Himself the
sins of men that He may atone for them.

The Agony in the Garden

Today's picture shows the Agony in the Garden.[21] After the Last Supper, when Jesus washed the Apostles' feet and instituted the Blessed Sacrament, after Judas went to sell Him to the Jews, they all went to the olive garden on a hill where Jesus often prayed at night.[22] He said His soul was sorrowful, even unto death. He left all but three of the Apostles outside the garden and took in with Him Peter and James and John, and told them to keep awake while He prayed a little way off.

Then He knelt down and began to go into an agony, which means a struggle; for He was struggling to make His own human heart, which feared suffering and shame, go along with the will of His Father in Heaven, and to make His human weakness take upon itself the dreadful weight of the world's sin and its punishment. The struggle was so great and He made such great acts of love with His heart that His sacred blood came through His skin like sweat.

Three times He went to visit the three Apostles, and each time, He found them sleeping. The first time, He said to them, "Watch and pray."

[21] You can read more about Jesus' agony in Matthew 26:30-45, Mark 14:32-41, and Luke 22:39-46.

[22] Matthew 26:20-30, Mark 14:18-26, Luke 22:14-39, and John 13:1-30 and 18:1.

The second time, He said to Peter, "Simon, couldst thou not watch one hour with me?"

Jesus thought about His Passion

In the picture, the three different parts of the agony are shown, one below another. Our Lord was alone in His agony; all the other figures in the picture (except the three Apostles in the top part) show the thoughts of Jesus. In the top part you see Jerusalem, all dark, standing for the sinful world; you see on the left Judas (his friend, whom He had loved well) coming to kiss Him so that the soldiers of the high priest would know whom to seize.[23] You see on the right His mother, Mary, and the holy women and other friends He would not see again in this world (except some of them from the Cross). You see the Cross, close to Jesus, for He is thinking of His Passion, step by step: all the loss, all the hatred, all the insults and cruelties, all the shame and disgrace, all the loneliness, and the torture and death. He says, "Father, let this chalice [that is, this suffering] pass away from me; yet not my will but Thine be done." Because there is no answer, He offers Himself to bear the Passion and to be obedient unto death.

Jesus took the world's sins upon Himself

In the middle of the picture you see the thoughts of Jesus in the second part of His agony. He remembers that His Father cannot let His own Son suffer the Passion, the punishment of sin, unless He sees the Son with the sins of the world upon Him. So Jesus must take our sins upon Him, and

---

[23] Matthew 26:47-50, Mark 14:43-46, and Luke 22:47-48.

the shame and horror of this is worse than anything He has felt before. In the picture, sin is like a great rock falling upon Him, and at the sides are shown some of the worst of men's sins: on the left, cruelty and murder and despair, and underneath, sacrilege; on the right, the worship of money, and hatred and blasphemy (some men trampling on a crucifix); and there is a picture of souls in Hell that would not let themselves be saved by the love of Jesus Christ. Now He says, "Father, if it be possible, let this chalice pass from me, yet not my will but Thine be done."

Jesus' heart was broken by those who did not love Him

When Jesus kneels down at the third part of His agony, He can see only a great, black cloud of sin between Himself and His Father. There is nowhere to look but at men He is going to save by His Cross. And what does He see? He sees all the pagans who do not know Him, even now, because there are not enough priests to convert them; He sees the men who have known Him and His great love and yet hate Him, like persecutors of the Church, and like all hardened sinners. He sees those who pretend to love Him, but follow Him in a cold, half-hearted, cowardly way. And now the heart of Jesus is breaking with this last grief, the heaviest of all for His human heart. He says, "Father, all things are possible to Thee; remove this chalice from me; but not what I will, but what Thou wilt."

And now His Father sends an angel to "strengthen Him." Perhaps the angel showed Him a vision of the big and little saints who would love Him truly and be saved by His Cross and by the Blessed Sacrament. You can recognize some of the saints in the picture by their clothes. Pray to these saints to help you respond to the love of Jesus Christ and His heavenly Father, who let Him die for us.

⚜

Yes or No?

1. Was Jesus Christ very sorrowful when He
began to pray in the olive garden?

2. Was He sad and afraid?

3. Did His being God prevent His human heart
from suffering in these ways?

4. Did it prevent His having a great agony, or struggle?

5. Was it a struggle to make His human heart go the way of
His Father's will, the way of His Passion and death?

6. Was the thought of His Passion, the scourging and
crowning and all the rest, dreadful to Him?

7. Did He hesitate for one moment about doing his Father's will?

8. Was Jesus sad to leave His Mother and His friends the Apostles?

9. Was He sad that His friend Judas would betray Him?

10. Did Jesus take all our sins upon Himself?

11. Could His Father have let Him suffer and die if
Jesus had not taken our sins upon Himself?

12. Did all this sin make a great load of
shame upon the heart of Jesus?

13. Did it seem like a dark cloud between Him and His Father?

14. Then did Jesus offer Himself with all His
heart to make up for our sins?

15. Before the angel came to Him, did Jesus get any
comfort by thinking of how men would love Him
for all He was doing for them?

16. Was He sad to think of all the pagans and all the wicked
men who would hate Him and His Church, and all the
Christians who would not love Him completely?

17. Was it to strengthen His breaking heart that the angel was sent?

18. Was Jesus strengthened by looking at all the souls who
would remember His Passion and thank Him for it and
love Him truly and make sacrifices with Him?

(13 yeses and 5 noes)

The Cross of Jesus is the way,
the life, and the light of the whole world.

The Cross of Jesus

The death of Jesus is the life of the world. The Cross of Jesus is God's greatest gift to men. The Cross of Jesus is the infinite love of God, shining on the earth and changing its darkness to light.

The Cross of Jesus is the only way to God

The Cross of Jesus is a great road or ladder by which all men can climb up to God; there is no other way to go; all who love Jesus go this way. Look at them on the Cross with Jesus: our Lady herself, first of all, and St. John the Baptist and St. Catherine[24] and the Curé of Ars[25] and St. Francis;[26] all the big and little saints and the souls in Purgatory and all who are on the way to Heaven. At the very foot you see some crusaders beginning to go up this royal road.

The Cross of Jesus is like a fruitful vine

The Cross of Jesus is like a great vine-tree planted in the earth and growing right into Heaven. Jesus is the vine, and those who love Him

---

[24] Possibly St. Catherine of Siena (c. 1347-1380). — Ed.

[25] St. John Vianney (1786-1859).

[26] St. Francis of Assisi (c. 1181-1226).

are the branches.[27] And the juice of the grapes is the Precious Blood of Jesus, and mingled with it is the blood of the martyrs, who die for Him. And the Precious Blood pours out over all the earth and makes the earth fruitful, so that there is a great harvest of souls for priests to gather in; and these souls from all different countries go to the Cross of Jesus, which is the gate of Heaven.

The Cross of Jesus is His throne

The Cross of Jesus is the throne of Jesus, the great King and the great High Priest, who offers up to God forever the perfect sacrifice of Himself (and along with Himself, those who love Him and come to His Cross). This great sacrifice is the same as the Sacrifice of the Mass. All these things you can see in the picture.

The Cross of Jesus leads to eternal happiness

The Cross of Jesus is the happiness and the blessedness of all the saints in Heaven forever and ever. St. John, in his vision of Heaven, saw "the Lamb standing, as it were slain";[28] and he says that Heaven has no need of the sun nor of the moon to shine in it because "the Lamb is the lamp thereof."[29] (Jesus is called the Lamb of God because He was sacrificed like the lambs at the time of the Passover in the Old Testament.[30]) So, in the picture you see a bright star over the Cross, and under that, the crown of glory, which is the crown of Jesus and all His saints in Heaven.

[27] John 15:5.

[28] Revelation 5:6.

[29] Revelation 21:23.

[30] Exodus 12:21-27.

The lesson of the picture is that the only way to Heaven is by the Cross of Jesus. Now, the Cross means suffering. But it is suffering with Jesus, and therefore a suffering that is blessed and happy, because it is for His sake, just as His suffering is for our sake, and because at the end, all this suffering is turned into joy and peace.

Yes or No?

1. Did Jesus Christ die on the Cross so that we might live forever in Heaven?

2. Is the Cross of Jesus like a great road or ladder leading to Heaven?

3. Is there any other way to Heaven except by the Cross of Jesus?

4. Can we go to Heaven by the Cross of Jesus without taking up our own crosses and following Him?

5. Did any of the saints refuse to suffer for Jesus' sake?

6. Did this suffering turn into joy?

7. Was that because they suffered along with Jesus?

8. Is the Cross of Jesus like a great vine, and His Precious Blood like the juice of the grapes?

9. Does the Precious Blood flow down and make the earth fruitful, so that there is a harvest of souls?

10. Is the Cross of Jesus like the throne of a great king, and like an altar on which Jesus, the great High Priest, offers Himself as a perfect sacrifice to God?

11. Is it a different sacrifice from the Sacrifice of the Mass?

(7 yeses and 4 noes)

Jesus, risen from the dead, comforts
and strengthens His faithful friends.

Jesus the Consoler

W hen Jesus rose from the grave, all glorious and happy, He did not go straight back to His Father in Heaven because He wished to have time to console and comfort His Mother and the holy women and His disciples. The parts of the Gospels that tell about the forty days Jesus stayed on earth after His Resurrection are like a little glimpse of Heaven, where Jesus Himself will console us and give us joy.[31]

The Gospels don't tell about how Jesus met His Mother after His Resurrection; that was too private and holy. But the little picture in the circle under the figure of Jesus rising from the dead will help you to think about it. You see the cradle in which Mary once nursed Him, and you see the carpenter's bench where He worked hard under the direction of St. Joseph.

Jesus increases faith

The pictures in the other four circles show Jesus teaching and strengthening souls in four different ways. One of them needed more faith. It was St. Thomas; he dared to say he would not believe Jesus was alive, even though the others had told him so, unless he put his fingers into the wounds. So

---

[31] Matthew 28:16-20, Mark 16:9-14, Luke 24:13-50, and John 20:11-30 and 21:1-23.

Jesus made him do this, and then told him how blessed it is to believe even when you have not seen.[32]

Jesus renews hope

The next were Cleophas and his friend, who ran away from Jerusalem after the Crucifixion, giving up all hope. Jesus met them on the road; they did not know Him, but He showed them how the prophets had said that He would suffer and die and "so enter into his glory." And then in the inn, He gave them Communion and they knew Him, and were full of joy and hope and courage all in a moment.[33]

Jesus deepens love

The third was Mary Magdalene, who loved Him so much, but not yet in the highest way; she needed to be helped about charity, or the spiritual love of God. She cried so much that she couldn't recognize Jesus, and then she wanted to hold Him tightly, as if He were going to escape. Jesus helped her by giving her something to do for Him, although it meant going away from Him; He sent her to bring a message to the Apostles.[34]

Jesus perfects contrition

The last was St. Peter, who had denied our Lord during the Passion. He was full of contrition, but his contrition was too sad and bitter, and he thought he couldn't be taken back into full favor with Jesus again. Jesus helped him by asking him three times in front of the other Apostles,

---

[32] John 20:24-29.

[33] Luke 24:13-35.

[34] John 20:11-17.

"Simon, lovest thou Me?" And each time Peter said, "Yes, Lord," Jesus said, "Feed my lambs," and the third time, "Feed my sheep." Jesus said this to show that Peter was still the chief shepherd even over the other Apostles.[35]

Jesus' death gives life to the world

The rest of the picture is easy to understand. The fresh new flowers all around are to show the new life that Jesus, by His death, gives to the world and to each of us if we take that life and keep it. In the figure of Jesus you see the grave cloths to remind you that He really died for us; now He is casting them off forever. Behind His head is the figure of the Cross, but now it is a glorious shining light. At His feet are two angels who have set two burning lamps before Him. You may take these two lamps for your body and your soul, which should always live in the presence of Jesus and burn in His honor, because He gave His body and soul for us.

Yes or No?

1. Did Jesus go straight back to Heaven when He had risen from the grave?

2. Was it for His own sake that He still stayed on earth for forty days?

3. Was it to console His Mother and all those who had been true to Him?

4. Was it to strengthen them too?

---

[35] John 21:15-17.

5. Did He strengthen different persons especially in faith, in hope, in love or charity, and in contrition?

6. Did they get strength from Jesus without having to do anything themselves?

7. Was St. Thomas more blessed than the others because He put his fingers into the wounds of Jesus?

8. Did Cleophas have to think about the prophecies about Jesus before he was made strong in hope?

9. Did Mary Magdalene have to leave our Lord in order to learn how to love Him perfectly?

10. Did St. Peter have to declare his love of Jesus humbly in front of the others to be made perfect in his contrition?

(6 yeses and 4 noes)

Take, O Lord, and accept all my liberty,
my memory, my mind, and all my will.

How to Love God

Now comes the end of this book on how to love God. And the first thing we are to think of is that love is shown in deeds, not in words. And then we are to think how anyone who loves another tries to give him everything he can that the other needs. Now we should think how God does this to us.

Say a little prayer to God to ask Him to teach you to love Him, and then look at the picture. In the picture, you are standing before God and all His angels and saints, with your hands held up to Him. And God is standing in a sort of pavilion, or tent, made of all the things God has created.

God gives me many gifts

Now look at God's garments; and look first at the long stole, or scapular, that is hanging straight down in the middle. On this are shown all the greatest gifts God has given you. At the top is a picture of your soul being put into your body by God when you were first made. Then there is a picture of how He saved you from sin and Hell by becoming man and dying on the Cross. Then there is a picture of the Church that Jesus Christ founded for your sake, with seven towers for the seven sacraments. Then you see the greatest of these sacraments, the Holy Eucharist, in which God gives Himself to you to be the food of your soul.

God comes close to me in His gifts

God doesn't send you these gifts from a long way off. Rather, in these gifts, He comes close to you. He comes to you in Jesus Christ, who is God; He comes to you in the Church; He comes to you in the Blessed Sacrament. But He comes to you also in the very gift of your body and soul; and He lives in your body and soul by His power, making you able to breathe and live and remember and think and do all the things you can do.

And God lives by His love not only in you, but in all His creatures. And He does this in order to come close to you, because He loves you. That is why the picture shows God standing in the pavilion of the world He has made. Look at all the things drawn there and say, "In the future, they shall always remind me of God."

God's work is a "labor of love"

God's gifts are not like the gifts of a very rich man, which cost him nothing; for although God can do all things, He does them out of love, and each thing He does is "a labor of love."[36] In His gifts to you, God works for you; and in the end, His work for us has cost Him a great deal: it has cost Him the death of His only Son on the Cross. In the picture, to remind you that God labors in love for us, the six days' work of the creation are shown on the inner garment of God, under the long stole. At the top is the first day,

---

[36] 1 Thessalonians 1:3.

when light was made, and so on downward to the creation of Adam and Eve.

God shares His divine possessions with me

There is one last, harder thought to help us to love God. You know that in each of us there is some goodness, but not perfect goodness like God's; and there is some wisdom, although perhaps there is not much at first; and there is some knowledge and some power and some truth. And these are the most precious things we have. Where did they come from? Did we get goodness and wisdom and the rest by ourselves? No, it all came flowing down into us out of the infinite goodness and power and wisdom and knowledge and truth of God! He shares His divine possessions with us, as far as we are able to share them! How good God is! All this is shown in the picture, on God's outer cloak, in the form of spirits of flame bringing down sparks of God's goodness.

And now you will wish to respond to God's great love; not by words, but by deeds and gifts. If you turn to the picture, you will see that the crusader, because he has nothing else to give, has given God his heart. He has thrown it right up to God, and you see that little heart quite close to God's face. It is this that God is looking at. And while he gives God his whole heart, this is what the crusader says:

"Take, O Lord, and accept all my liberty, my memory, my understanding, and all my will, everything that is in me or belongs to me. You gave me all these things; to You, O Lord, I give them back. They are all Yours; make use of them just as You wish! Give to me Your love and Your grace; these are enough for me."

This prayer was made by St. Ignatius; it is a good prayer to learn by heart.

⚬

Yes or No?

1. Is love shown best by words?

2. Is it shown best by deeds?

3. If anyone truly loves, does he give all
he can to the one he loves?

4. Has God given us all He possibly can give?

5. Has He given us our own body and soul?

6. Has He given us His only Son, Jesus Christ, to die for us?

7. Do we have Him still in the Church
and in the Blessed Sacrament?

8. Does God give us His gifts from a long way off?

9. Does He dwell in His gifts and come close to us?

10. Does God labor for us and serve us in all
the wonderful works of His creation?

11. Does He do all this out of love?

12. Did the little bits of goodness or wisdom or
knowledge or power that I find in myself
come to be there of themselves?

13. Did I make them?

14. Are they like sparks from God's goodness
and knowledge and power and wisdom that
have come down into my soul?

15. Can I give God something He wants
in return for all this?

16. Is it my heart?

17. Do you know a prayer by which to make this gift?

18. Have you learned it by heart?

(12 yeses, 4 noes, and 2 maybes)

Appendices

A closer look at the pictures

Now that you have finished reading this book, it's time to take a closer look at the pictures. They are full of surprises that you will enjoy finding. After you have looked more closely at the pictures, you will understand even more about the chapters you have read.

MADE FOR GOD

God made me for Himself, and He made all other things to get me to Him.

1. In this picture are the Latin words LAUS DEO,
   meaning "praise to God." Can you find them?

2. God filled the universe with wonderful things,
   from tiny insects to huge stars. How many
   of these can you find in the picture?

A lizard

A swallow

A bird's nest

Sparrows

A spider
in a web

Fire

A puppy

A squirrel

A rabbit

A stag

3. Look closely and see if you can find
   these people in the picture.

A little child
with a balloon

A monk reading
to children

A devil
throwing rocks

A crusader
fixing a sword

An angel
with a shield

A shepherd

A guardian
angel protecting
a hurt crusader

THE BEST WAY OF LIFE

The best kind of life is the one that will take me to Heaven.

1. In the picture are people at work and at play. Can you find these?

A boy playing a pipe

A painter

A policeman

A woman walking her dog

2. Honor and riches are not good if they lead you away from God. Here is someone who prefers honor to God and someone who is burdened by riches. Can you find them in the picture?

3. Can you find these crusaders who have left riches and honor behind them to follow Jesus?

4. Try to find the church bell in this picture.

5. Look at the many different buildings in the picture. Can you find these two very different homes?

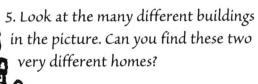

6. In Heaven this baby is carrying a star. Do you see him?

THE THREE SINS

Sin is the only evil. It ruined some of the angels and Adam and may ruin me.

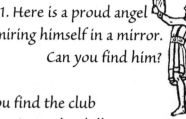

1. Here is a proud angel admiring himself in a mirror. Can you find him?

2. Can you find the club that Cain used to kill his brother Abel?

3. Look for this shovel in the picture.

4. There are three serpents in this picture. Can you find them?

5. What are the bad angels doing after being thrown out of Heaven? Do you see the ones breaking the trees and leaving sharp thorns and rocks instead?

6. Can you find the devil with a pig's head?

7. Look at the animals in the Garden of Eden (at the upper left) with Adam and Eve before they disobeyed God. Can you find the animal near Adam and Eve AFTER they sinned?

8. Find this smiling devil.

9. Can you find this man reaching out to God in his sorrow?

10. There are three crosses in this picture. Can you find them all?

MY OWN SINS

God has done all He can for me, and yet I have sinned against Him.

1. The dove is a symbol of the Holy Spirit. Can you find it?

2. Look carefully at the left middle part of the picture. Do you see the angel playing a pipe? What kind of animal is the angel leading to God? How many more of these animals can you find in the picture?

3. At the bottom of the picture are seven ugly trolls. These represent the sins of pride, sloth, hate, despair, lust, envy, and greed. Can you find each one in the picture?

HATE leads to murder

LUST is like a wild beast

PRIDE is self-obsessed

GREED never shares

ENVY wants what someone else has

DESPAIR gives up hope

SLOTH never does anything

4. Wheat and grapes are symbols of the Eucharist. Can you find them in the picture?

A grapevine

5. These scary heads are part of the gates of Hell. Would you like to go through them?

A songbird

6. The earth is full of life and beauty. Find these signs of God's goodness.

A water lily

A butterfly

A frog

A lamb

An iris

A duck

Rabbits

A cow

An angel tending flowers

75

THE CALL OF A KING

Jesus calls you to fight by His side. How do you answer Him?

1. Here are some people who have chosen not to follow Jesus. Can you find them in the picture?

Pagans worshiping an idol

A king who makes people his slaves

A coward

2. The fight against sin can be hard. Here is a brave crusader who has been wounded. Look for him in the picture. Can you find others who are fighting on Jesus' side?

3. Sometimes people do bad things because other people tell them to. Find this man who is beating a prisoner for the cruel king.

4. The picture shows some of the holy places where Jesus lived and taught. Look for these places where He was born and where He died.

Bethlehem

Jerusalem

Calvary

THE INCARNATION

The Son of God became man to save men from sin and lead them to Heaven.

1. The angel Gabriel told Mary that she would be the mother of Jesus. Can you find Gabriel in this picture?

2. Can you find the star of Bethlehem? Do you remember who followed the star to find Jesus? (Read Matthew 2:1-2.)

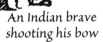

3. Pagans are people who worship idols, which are false gods. Can you find the statues of pagan idols in this picture? Now see how many more idols you can find in the other pictures in this book.

4. Jesus came to save people from all around the world and throughout all of history. Look for some of these ancient people who are doing interesting things.

A rich Roman lady at a family party

A caveman painting a picture

An Indian brave shooting his bow

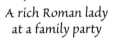

An Egyptian with a camel

A man fishing with a spear

A Roman soldier standing guard

People driving a dogsled

Bandits attacking a caravan

THE TWO STANDARDS

Satan says: greed, vainglory, pride. Christ says: poverty, contempt, humility.

1. Can you find the man who symbolizes time in the picture?
He is holding a scythe and an hourglass.

2. The devils have taken some proud people
as their prisoners. How many have been
chained by the devils? How many
devils are using nets to catch people?

3. Why are these devils so unhappy? Look
at the picture and find what's making
them angry.

4. At the top right of the
picture is a poor man with a crutch
asking for help from a rich man.
What is the rich man doing?

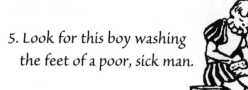

5. Look for this boy washing
the feet of a poor, sick man.

6. Can you find a skull?

7. See if you can find this jester.

THE ELECTION

I must choose my state of life according to God's glory and my salvation.

1. We hang crucifixes in our homes to remind us of Jesus' love for us. Find this crucifix in the picture. Then find another crucifix hanging on a wall in the picture.

2. Find the book on its stand.

3. The candle stands for faith. Find this one, and then look for the other candlesticks in the picture.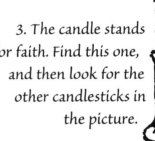

4. This balance is used to weigh things. Can you find it?

5. See if you can find this devil with wings.

6. Look for this crusader who is asking God for help and guidance in choosing what to do when he grows up.

7. Did you find all three of the treasure chests the devil is trying to give to the crusader? Now find the bag that the crusader is taking on his journey.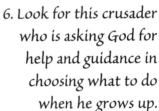

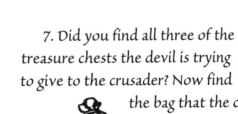

8. Look closely at the picture of St. Matthew following Jesus. What is he doing with his money?

THE AGONY IN THE GARDEN

Jesus Christ takes on Himself the sins of men that He may atone for them.

1. Peter, James, and John were supposed to watch with Jesus, but they fell asleep instead. Can you find two of these Apostles sleeping?

2. This golden cup is called a chalice. Can you find it in the picture?

3. Here are some things you will see in church:
   Lectionary — the book containing readings for Mass
   Candles — these are often made of beeswax
   Tabernacle — a place where the Eucharist is kept
   Can you find them in the picture?

4. There are lots of sharp, thorny cactus plants in this picture. How many can you find?

5. Here are people worshiping an idol. Can you find them? Do they look happy?

6. Jesus gave Peter the keys of the kingdom of Heaven. Can you find St. Peter with a key?

7. Can you find Jesus on the Cross?

THE CROSS OF JESUS

The Cross of Jesus is the way, the life, and the light of the whole world.

1. The saints know that the Cross of Jesus is the way to Heaven. Can you find these saints in the picture?

St. John the Baptist

St. John Vianney (the Curé of Ars)

Our Lady

St. Sebastian

St. Thomas More

St. Francis of Assisi

2. The Cross of Jesus saves people from all over the world and throughout all of history. Look for these people asking Jesus to save them.

3. This is a sheaf of wheat. How many sheaves can you find? How many people are harvesting them?

4. The harvest of wheat stands for the work of the Church. Can you find these people working for God?

A nun teaching children

A priest celebrating Mass, and an altar boy ringing the bells

5. Even on the Cross, Jesus is still a king. Can you find His crown?

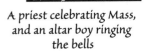

JESUS THE CONSOLER

Jesus, risen from the dead, comforts and strengthens His faithful friends.

1. Each of these pictures shows a different part of the Holy Land where Jesus visited His friends: the upper room, the road to Emmaus, the garden of the Resurrection, and the Sea of Tiberias. Can you match the places with the pictures?

2. The trees in this picture seem bare — but look closely at them. Do you see the buds and the tiny leaves starting to grow? These are signs of new life.

3. In Jesus' time, people used oil lamps for light. Can you find two in the picture?

4. These flowers are called daffodils. How many daffodil blossoms can you find?

HOW TO LOVE GOD

Take, O Lord, and accept all my liberty, my memory, my mind, and all my will.

1. Can you find these Latin words that tell what God is?

SCIENTIA = knowledge   BONITAS = goodness

SAPIENTIA = wisdom   JUSTITIA = justice

VERITAS = truth   POTESTAS = power

MISERICORDIA = mercy

2. These angels are called seraphim. They look like flames because their love for God is so strong and pure. How many seraphim can you find?

Stars

Planets

The moon

Gifts in the sky

Clouds

Birds

3. God reveals Himself to us in His gifts. Look for these gifts in the picture.

Our homes
Here is a map of the artist's country, Great Britain. What country do you live in?

Gifts on the land and in the sea

Animals

Mountains

Fish

Trees and plants

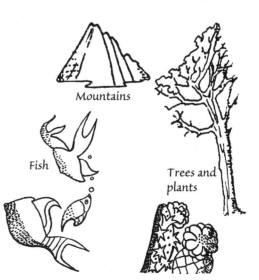

Geoffrey Bliss, S.J.

Geoffrey Bliss (1874-1952) was a Jesuit priest, writer, and teacher. Born in Oxford, England, he was one of twelve children. After attending school in England, he entered the Society of Jesus at age 18.

Fr. Bliss spent most of his priesthood spreading devotion to the Sacred Heart of Jesus. In 1920, he became the editor of the magazine the MESSENGER OF THE SACRED HEART. He was also named the National Secretary of the Apostleship of Prayer, an organization that was dedicated to promoting devotion to the Sacred Heart, especially among young people. To assist this movement, Fr. Bliss began a magazine called the CHILDREN'S MESSENGER in 1928. Caryll Houselander, a writer and artist, contributed articles and illustrations to the magazine.

Fr. Bliss loved poetry, beauty, and order. With childlike eyes, he was able to see God's presence in the wonders of creation. His writings have shown many young people how to find God's presence in their lives and how to reach the kingdom of Heaven.

Caryll Houselander

Frances Caryll Houselander (1901-1954) was born in Bath, England, in 1901. Caryll, as she is known, and her sister were baptized into the Catholic Church in 1907. Her parents separated when she was nine years old. She was then sent to convent schools until she was sixteen. Personal troubles led her away from the Catholic Church for a while. During these years, she went to St. John's Wood Art School in London. She worked at many jobs and tried other religions. In her twenties, she returned to the Catholic Church. She worked for the Church as a painter and woodcarver.

Caryll Houselander wrote articles and drew pictures for the CHILDREN'S MESSENGER. She also wrote articles for THE GRAIL MAGAZINE. Some of these were printed in her first book, THIS WAR IS THE PASSION, which was published in 1941, during World War II. Houselander wrote many books in her lifetime. A ROCKING-HORSE CATHOLIC tells the story of her childhood and youth. Many have read her book THE REED OF GOD, which is about the Virgin Mary.

Caryll Houselander saw the image of Jesus in all men, women, and children. She served the Catholic Church with joy. Her writings have helped many Christians to love Jesus more and become more like Him.

Sophia Institute Press®

Sophia Institute is a nonprofit institution that seeks to restore man's knowledge of eternal truth, including man's knowledge of his own nature, his relation to other persons, and his relation to God.

We publish translations of foreign works to make them accessible for the first time to English-speaking readers. We bring back into print books that have been long out of print. And we publish important new books that fulfill the ideals of Sophia Institute. These books afford readers a rich source of the enduring wisdom of mankind.

Your generosity can help us provide the public with editions of works containing the enduring wisdom of the ages. Please send your tax-deductible contribution to the address below.

For a free catalog, call:
Toll-free: 1-800-888-9344

or write:
Sophia Institute Press®
Box 5284
Manchester, NH 03108

Sophia Institute is a tax-exempt institution
as defined by the Internal Revenue Code,
Section 501(c)(3). Tax I.D. 22-2548708.